First World War
and Army of Occupation
War Diary
France, Belgium and Germany

32 DIVISION
Divisional Troops
164 Brigade Royal Field Artillery
29 December 1915 - 1 September 1916

WO95/2380/5

The Naval & Military Press Ltd
www.nmarchive.com
Published in association with The National Archives

Published by

The Naval & Military Press Ltd

Unit 10 Ridgewood Industrial Park,

Uckfield, East Sussex,

TN22 5QE England

Tel: +44 (0) 1825 749494

www.naval-military-press.com

www.nmarchive.com

This diary has been reprinted in facsimile from the original. Any imperfections are inevitably reproduced and the quality may fall short of modern type and cartographic standards.

© Crown Copyright
Images reproduced by permission of The National Archives, London, England, 2015.

Contents

Document type	Place/Title	Date From	Date To
Heading	32nd Division Divl Artillery 164th (Howitzer) Bde R.F.A. Jan-Sep 1916 Broken Up.		
Heading	32nd Divisional Artillery. 164th (Howitzer) Brigade R.F.A. January 1916 (29.12.1915 to 31.1.1916) Sep 16		
War Diary	Sutton Mandeville Camp Wilts.	29/12/1915	29/12/1915
War Diary	Salisbury.	29/12/1915	29/12/1915
War Diary	Southampton.	30/12/1915	30/12/1915
War Diary	L. Havre.	31/12/1915	31/12/1915
War Diary	Tisbury.	30/12/1915	30/12/1915
War Diary	Southampton.	31/12/1915	31/12/1915
War Diary	L. Havre.	01/01/1916	02/01/1916
War Diary	St. Sauveur.	05/01/1916	05/01/1916
War Diary	St. Sauveur.	05/01/1916	07/01/1916
War Diary	St. Sauveur.	05/01/1916	06/01/1916
War Diary	St. Sauveur.	05/01/1916	07/01/1916
War Diary	Warloy.	12/01/1916	12/01/1916
War Diary		07/01/1916	19/01/1916
War Diary	Meauze.	09/01/1916	09/01/1916
War Diary	Warloy.	22/01/1916	22/01/1916
War Diary	Martinsart.	22/01/1916	23/01/1916
War Diary	Warloy.	24/01/1916	24/01/1916
War Diary	Martinsart.	27/01/1916	27/01/1916
War Diary	Warloy.	29/01/1916	31/01/1916
Heading	32nd Divisional Artillery. 164th (Howitzer) Brigade R.F.A. February 1916.		
War Diary	Warloy.	01/02/1916	13/02/1916
War Diary	Baizieux.	14/02/1916	16/02/1916
War Diary	Albert.	20/02/1916	29/02/1916
Heading	32nd Divisional Artillery. 164th (Howitzer) Brigade R.F.A. March 1916.		
War Diary	Albert.	01/03/1916	26/03/1916
War Diary		02/03/1916	30/03/1916
War Diary		01/03/1916	26/03/1916
War Diary		18/03/1916	18/03/1916
Heading	32nd Divisional Artillery. 164th (Howitzer) Brigade R.F.A. April 1916.		
War Diary	Meaulte.	07/04/1918	15/04/1918
War Diary	Albert.	06/04/1916	07/04/1916
War Diary	Martinsart.	08/04/1916	25/04/1916
War Diary	Aveluy.	25/04/1916	25/04/1916
Heading	32nd Divisional Artillery. 16th (Howitzer) Brigade R.F.A. May 1916.		
Heading	32nd Divisional Artillery. 164th (Howitzer) Brigade R.F.A. May 1916.		
Miscellaneous	To Office Change R.K. Records Base.		
War Diary	Albert.	01/05/1916	31/05/1916
Heading	32nd Divisional Artillery 164th Brigade. Royal Field Artillery. June 1916.		
War Diary	Albert.	00/06/1916	00/06/1916

Heading	War Diary Headquarters, 164th Brigade, R.F.A. (32nd Division) July 1916.		
War Diary	Aveluy Neighborhood.	01/07/1916	29/07/1916
Heading	32nd Divisional Artillery. 164th Brigade (Howitzer) R.F.A. August 1916.		
War Diary	Lapugnoy.	01/08/1916	26/08/1916
Heading	32nd Divisional Artillery. The Brigade Was Broken Up 17.9.16 164th (Howitzer) Brigade R.F.A. September 1916.		
War Diary	Philosophe.	01/09/1916	01/09/1916

32ND DIVISION
DIVL ARTILLERY

164TH (HOWITZER) BDE R.F.A.
JAN-SEP 1916

BROKEN UP

32nd Divisional Artillery.

164th (Howitzer) BRIGADE R. F. A.

JANUARY 1 9 1 6

(29.12.1915 to 31.1.1916)

Sep 16

16th Howitzer Brigade R.F.A. WAR DIARY Period 29/1/15 to 31/1/16

INTELLIGENCE SUMMARY

(Erase heading not required)

16th (HOWITZER) BRIGADE
Army Form C. 2118
31 JAN 1916
ROYAL FIELD ARTILLERY

Place	Date	Hour	Summary of Events and Information	Remarks and references to Appendices
SUTTON MANDEVILLE CAMP WILTS.	29/1/15		Brigade placed under orders for Active Service.	

Officers:
- MAJOR D.M. TWEEDIE. D.S.O. — Brigade Commander. R.F.A.
- CAPTAIN R.O. POWELL. R.F.A. — Adjutant
- 2/Lieut H.M. TAYLOR. R.F.A. — Orderly Officer } Headquarters 16th Brigade R.F.A.
- Lieutenant M.N. CHILD. R.A.M.C. — Medical Officer

A/16th Brigade R.F.A.
- CAPTAIN H.J. CALNAN. R.F.A.
- Lieutenant G.E. SAMUELS
- 2/Lieut A.L. STIRLING
- — A. RHODES

B/16th Brigade R.F.A.
- CAPTAIN E. PEASE-WATKIN. R.F.A.
- Lieutenant C.E. BURGESS
- 2/Lieut C.D. LEYDALL
- — J.W. BUCKLEY

C/16th Brigade R.F.A.
- CAPTAIN ...
- Lieutenant C.C. DRABBLE R.F.A.
- 2/Lieut G.H. WIDGERY
- — R. DUNBAR
- — J.C. POOLE

D/16th Brigade R.F.A.
- CAPTAIN N.R.C. TENISON R.F.A.
- Lieutenant E. BUCKLE
- 2/Lieut M.D. LITTLEWOOD
- — A.W. POLDEN

BAC/16th Brigade R.F.A.
- CAPTAIN H.C. WORRALL R.F.A.
- Lieutenant E. HART
- 2/Lieut A. ISHERWOOD

691 N.C.O's + men, 16 Guns, 48 A.S. Ammunition Wagons, 667 Horses

Army Form C. 2118.

WAR DIARY
or
INTELLIGENCE SUMMARY.
(Erase heading not required.)

Instructions regarding War Diaries and Intelligence Summaries are contained in F. S. Regs., Part II. and the Staff Manual respectively. Title pages will be prepared in manuscript.

Place	Date	Hour	Summary of Events and Information	Remarks and references to Appendices
SALISBURY	29/1/15	6.30 p.m.	(B/164 Brigade & B.A.C./164 Brigade R.F.A.) Entrained for Southampton and embarked on S/S ARCHIMEDES	
SOUTHAMPTON	30/1/15	11.30 p.m.	Sailed.	
L. HAVRE	31/1/15	7 a.m.	Disembarked & marched to Quarters in No 2 Camp at SANVIC	
TISBURY	30/1/15	12 a.m.	(Headquarters A, C, & D,/164 Brigade R.F.A.) Entrained for Southampton and embarked on S/S BELLEROPHON	
SOUTHAMPTON	31/1/15	4 p.m.	Sailed.	
L. HAVRE	1/4/16	9 a.m.	Disembarked & marched to Quarters in No 2 Camp at SANVIC	
L. HAVRE	2/1/16	part day & night	The whole Brigade entrained for LONGEAU, detrained & marched to Billets at ST SAUVEUR.	
ST. SAUVEUR	5/2/16	8 a.m.	(A/164 Brigade R.F.A.) Marched to LAVIEVILLE drew ammunition and entered into action relieving AVELUY and AUTHUILLE, section formerly occupied by 2nd RENFREW BATTERY. N.5a?1 Sheet 57 d S.E. former.	
ST. SAUVEUR	5/2/16		(B/164 Brigade R.F.A.) Drew ammunition from CORBIE.	
	7/2/16		Marched to LAVIEVILLE. Picked up an auxt. commander of Ammunition & ordered into action at P.33 a.7½.2½. Sheet 57 d S.E., formerly occupied by D/55 BATTERY R.F.A.	

2353 Wt. W3544/1454 700,000 5/15 D. D. & L. A.D.S.S./Forms/C. 2118.

Army Form C. 2118.

WAR DIARY
or
INTELLIGENCE SUMMARY.
(Erase heading not required.)

Instructions regarding War Diaries and Intelligence Summaries are contained in F. S. Regs., Part II. and the Staff Manual respectively. Title pages will be prepared in manuscript.

Place	Date	Hour	Summary of Events and Information	Remarks and references to Appendices
ST. SAUVEUR	5/6		(C/164 Brigade R.F.A.) Drew Ammunition & marched to Toeux, thence on to MEAULT & attached to C/85 Battery R.F.A. & went into action at E.11.6.9.5. Sheet 62d France	
	6/6			
ST. SAUVEUR	5/6		(D/164 Brigade R.F.A.) Drew Ammunition & marched to LE NEUVILLE & attached to A/85 Battery R.F.A. & went into action at F.4.d.9.5. Sheet 62d. near ALBERT.	
ST. SAUVEUR	7/6		(B.A.C/164 Brigade R.F.A.) Drew Ammunition from CORBIE. Marched to CONTAY and took up Billets there.	
ST. SAUVEUR	7/6		(Headquarters/164 Brigade R.F.A.) Marched to MARLOY & made Headquarters there.	
MARLOY	12/6		The Wagon lines of the Brigade brought to MARLOY. B.A.C/164 Brigade to remain at CONTAY. The Batteries were under instructions of the Units to which they were attached, chiefly being supplied by Regulating Zones. (1" to 9")	
MEAULT	9/6		Captain R.O. POWELL took over Command of C Battery. 2/Lieut J.C. Tooke appointed Acting Adjutant.	
MARLOY	22/6		LIEUT COLONEL H. ALLCARD took on Command of the Brigade. MAJOR D.K. TWEEDIE took command of C. Battery. CAPTAIN R.O. POWELL resumed Action as Adjutant. 2/Lieut J.C. POOLE posted to C. BATTERY.	

Army Form C. 2118.

WAR DIARY
or
INTELLIGENCE SUMMARY.
(Erase heading not required.)

Instructions regarding War Diaries and Intelligence Summaries are contained in F. S. Regs., Part II. and the Staff Manual respectively. Title pages will be prepared in manuscript.

Place	Date	Hour	Summary of Events and Information	Remarks and references to Appendices
MARTINSART	22/10	4pm	The 164th Brigade R.F.A. joined in centrated shoot on THIEPVAL	(R 25 a 2.4.) Sheet 57d S.E. France
—	23/10		C & D Batteries commence preparing new positions to be occupied by them	
MAILLY	24/10		2/Lieutenant M.S. CHILTERN joined C Battery, 2/Lieutenant S.R. ALEXANDER joined posted to D Battery	
MARTINSART	27/10		The 164 Brigade R.F.A. joined in centrated shoot on Ferme du MOUQUET.	R 33 b 2.5 Sheet 57d S.E. France
MAILLY	29/10		A & B Batteries are occupying former positions of:-	(A) M.5.d.7.1. Sheet 57c S.E. FRANCE
				(B) P.33.d.7½.2½
			C & D Batteries occupying former positions of:-	(C) M.15.b.4.1.
				(D) M.14.a.3.2.
Warloy	31/10		On taking up positions A & C Batteries were allotted to Lt. Colonel Cottons Group (161 Brigade R.F.A.) B & D Batteries were allotted to Lt Colonel Bamberg's Group (155 Brigade R.F.A.)	

Thomp Savill
Lieut.-Col., R.F.A.
Commdg. 164th Bde. R.F.A.

32nd Divisional Artillery.

164th (Howitzer) BRIGADE R. F. A.

FEBRUARY 1 9 1 6

164 Howitzer Brigade R.F.A.   Period 1/2/16 to 29/2/16.

Army Form C. 2118.

WAR DIARY
or
INTELLIGENCE SUMMARY.
(Erase heading not required.)

Place	Date	Hour	Summary of Events and Information	Remarks and references to Appendices
WARLOY	1/2/16		Headquarters 164 Brigade R.F.A. situate at WARLOY. A/Battery occupying position W.5 d.7-1 Sheet 57D S.E. FRANCE. B/Battery occupying position T.33.2.7½-2½ Sheet 57D S.E. FRANCE. C & D Batteries fortifying positions. B.A.C./164 Brigade situate at CONTAY.	
	1–3/2/16		Generally quiet. A/Battery position shelled each day. No casualties or damage to equipment.	
	4–5/2/16		B/Battery fired in combined shoot on THIEPVAL. (R.25.2.4-4 Sheet 57D S.E. FRANCE) Enemy retaliated on Battery around but did no damage	
	8/2/16		Railroad aeroplanes active	
	9/2/16		Enemy make attack on F.2 sector using gas shells. A/Battery ordered to fire on hostile line. Enemy retaliated with 5.9's on Battery's position. Two men of C/Battery accidentally wounded.	
	10/2/16		Aeroplane active	
	11/2/16		Enemy shell AVELUY WOOD. One man of C/Battery gassed	
	12/2/16		Enemy shell MESNIL and fired 50 rounds in the vicinity of A/Battery's position. 2nd Lieut. W.D. LITTLEWOOD D/Battery evacuated.	
	13/2/16		A/Battery one casualty. B.A.C./164 Brigade move to BAIZIEUX.	
BAIZIEUX	14/2/16		B/164 Right Section found out of action & move to BAIZIEUX. Headquarters 164 move from WARLOY to BAIZIEUX.	

WAR DIARY
or
INTELLIGENCE SUMMARY.
(Erase heading not required.)

Army Form C. 2118.

Place	Date	Hour	Summary of Events and Information	Remarks and references to Appendices
BAIZIEUX	15/7		Left Section B/Battery co out of action and move to BAIZIEUX.	
	15-16/7		A & C Batteries fire on German front line & support trenches generally.	
	16/7		D/Battery transferred to 49 R.D. Division. C/Battery four casualties due to premature.	
ALBERT	20/7		C/Battery commence preparing new position at W.22.b.7.4. Sheet 57 D. S.E. FRANCE. Headquarters 164 Brigade move from BAIZIEUX to ALBERT. B/Battery still continue work at BAIZIEUX.	
	16-20/7			
	21/7		A/Battery co out of action and move to BAIZIEUX. B/Battery move from BAIZIEUX and occupy position vacated by A/Battery.	
	22/7		B & C Batteries form a combined shoot on Fme du MOUQUET and OVILLERS. A/Battery commenced digging new position at W.17.c.15-95. OVILLERS 2nd Ed. date 1-7-15. Sheet No. 57 D.	
	23/7		Quiet, snowing	
	24/7		2nd Lieut. N.F. STIRLING evacuated. 2nd Lieut. G.H. WIDGERY posted from C to A Battery for duty.	
	24- -28/7		Quiet, heavy snow	

Army Form C. 2118.

WAR DIARY
or
INTELLIGENCE SUMMARY.
(Erase heading not required.)

Instructions regarding War Diaries and Intelligence Summaries are contained in F. S. Regs., Part II. and the Staff Manual respectively. Title pages will be prepared in manuscript.

Place	Date	Hour	Summary of Events and Information	Remarks and references to Appendices
ALBERT.	28/2		Right Section C/Battery moved to new position at W.22.b.7.4. Sheet 57.D S.E. FRANCE	
	29/2		Left Section C/Battery moved to new position at W.22.b.7.4. Sheet 57.D S.E. FRANCE.	
			B/Battery and Left Section C/Battery joined in combined shoot on German trenches.	

H. Alcock
Lieut.-Col., R.F.A.
Commdg. 164th Bde. R.F.A.

32nd Divisional Artillery.

164th (Howitzer) BRIGADE R. F. A.

MARCH 1 9 1 6

164" Howitzer Brigade R.F.A.   Period 1/3/16 to 31/3/16

Army Form C. 2118.

WAR DIARY
or
INTELLIGENCE SUMMARY.
(Erase heading not required.)

Instructions regarding War Diaries and Intelligence Summaries are contained in F. S. Regs., Part II. and the Staff Manual respectively. Title pages will be prepared in manuscript.

Stamp: 164th (NORTHERN) HOWITZER BRIGADE * ROYAL FIELD ARTILLERY — No. 19 — 17 APR 1916

Place	Date	Hour	Summary of Events and Information	Remarks and references to Appendices
Albert	1/3/16		Headquarters of 164th Brigade R.F.A. situated at ALBERT.	
	3/3/16		A/Battery received orders to move into (Right Group) their new position occupied by D/85 Brigade R.F.A. at E.12.a.10.55 (Maj. Dillon 5yD.SE) A/Battery completes the move. Also took over the wagon lines of D/85 at MEAULTE. They took over the 4.5" Howitzer guns of D/85 which were left in action. Howitzer Rev's on to D/85.	
	26/3/16		2nd Lt Chevallier & men belonging to A/Batt. [?] ammunition; Dr Nute Lt McMahon who were attached to a working party at AVELUY, were slightly wounded by a shell which struck their billet.	
	2/3/16		B/Battery moves into new position in the district of ALBERT. Took part in a bombardment of enti. guns in CONTALMAISON.	
	17/3/16		G. Layard severely wounded & 5 Cannoniers slightly wounded by shell which burst in their billet at AVELUY. They were attached to a digging party near LA BOISSELLE fires on LA BOISSELLE trees on the Kerode Junction.	
	26/3/16			
	27/3/16		Took part in the raid on LA BOISSELLE fires on the Kerode Junction.	
	30/3/16		Lt. T. Fulcher R.F.A. S.R. joined Battery from C/6 Reserve Bde. R.F.A. Leeds. To course of gunnery. Weather all through the month has been fine, chiefly frost, snow, & [?] frosts.	

Army Form C. 2118.

WAR DIARY
or
INTELLIGENCE SUMMARY.
(Erase heading not required.)

Place	Date	Hour	Summary of Events and Information	Remarks and references to Appendices
	1 3/16		C/ Battery in action west of ALBERT.	
	9 3/16		The Battery joined in a combined shoot of the left Group Howrs on the Ennem	
			trenches in front of THIEPVAL.	
	15 3/16		The Battery was shelled heavily by Enemy 5.9"(Hows) owing to their close proximity	
			to an Anti-Aircraft section.	
	16 3/16		Battery moved to a new position which had been partly prepared by us A/Bde	
			& situated on the Railway close to AVELUY.	
	26 3/16		Shoot at Midnight in support of an Infantry raid on LA BOISSELLE.	
	18 3/16		Serjeant T Johnston was mortally wounded by a shell bursting over the gun	
			at the rear of Officers Billet.	
			The weather during the month has been consistently bad.	
			B+C. billetted at BAZIEUX.	

J. Vincent
Lieut. Col.
Commdg. 161st Bde. R.F.A.

32nd Divisional Artillery.

164th (Howitzer) BRIGADE R. F. A.

APRIL 1 9 1 6

162ⁿᵈ How. Bde. R.F.A.   Period 1/7/16 to 30/7/16

WAR DIARY or INTELLIGENCE SUMMARY

164 RFA VOL 4
XXII

Place	Date	Hour	Summary of Events and Information
Meaulte	7/7/16	7 P.M.	A/162 — Handed over Right Section to positions to 8 Div (53ʳᵈ Bde). Receives two howitzers. Section B at the wagon line. These How's appears to be of rather early date & in a rather bad condition. Left Section now out of action. Horses filled by a section from 21ˢᵗ Div. Whd. Batt. The Section at proceeded to Meaulte via or route, partly via El Sarnet, but proceeds to Senadin & Avelny, Mentinsart-Lenguevarat Roads to Touques wag section.
	12/7/16		2/Lt H Cockayne R.F.A. posts to Batt'y for 36 Div Sigs. He relieves Lt Sommets in charge of working party.
	15/7/16		Lt A Rhoda proceeds to Havernas as a Gunnery Officer.
			B/162
			The Left Section now from action at Albert & action at Mentinsart relieves the 35ᵗʰ Batt. R.F.A.
ALBERT	6/7/16		
	7/7/16		Right Section moves to Mentinsart.

WAR DIARY or INTELLIGENCE SUMMARY

Army Form C. 2118.

Place	Date	Hour	Summary of Events and Information	Remarks and references to Appendices
MARTINSART	8/7/16		B/161 Continued	
	9/7/16		2/Lt C.L.W. Hassarder joins the Batt. from the 32nd D.A.C.	
	18/7/16		2/Lt C Kendall joins the 32nd D.A.C.	
	22/7/16		Inspection of Batt. Guns by I.O.M.	
	25/7/16		After repairs his of our ammunition gun by two of the Guns	
			Arrived in a raid by the 17th H.L.I. and 283 B.X.	
			Lt. C.E. Burgess repaired a tear to England	
			C/161	
			The Batt. was in action during the whole month saw nothing unusual happened during the month with the exception of a raid by the Infantry on nights of 22/23. In which the Batt. cooperated by firing a Gas and Smoke Barrage through shots were carried out by Aeroplane Observation on Anti-Aircraft gun positions been prepared out. The follow officers joined the Batt. 2/Lt G.T. Davis RFA (T) 2/Lt C.S. Rice RFA (S.R.)	
AVELUY			Casualties - a Bomb. E Brown & wounded in action Gun. W Trompeter ~	
			[signature] Commdg R.F.A.

32nd Divisional Artillery.

164th (Howitzer) BRIGADE R.F.A.

M A Y 1 9 1 6

32nd Divisional Artillery.

164th (Howitzer) BRIGADE R.F.A.

M A Y 1 9 1 6

To/ Officer in Charge R.A. Records
                    Base.
═

Reference your note requesting us to forward to you the War Diary for May this was sent to you on the 4th June/16 but evidently failed to reach you. As the duplicates have been destroyed on account of moving quickly I have done what I can to give you a correct record.

C. Dabbh. Lt.   R.F.A.
Adjutant, 164 (Rotherham) Brigade R.F.A.

Army Form C. 2118.

XXXI WAR DIARY for May/16 164th Bde RFA Vol 5

INTELLIGENCE SUMMARY

(Erase heading not required.)

Place	Date	Hour	Summary of Events and Information	Remarks and references to Appendices
Alush	May 1/16 to 31		On the 4th May this H.Q. took over the control of the Artillery Group covering the 2 sub-sectors of the line known as the Cortewille & Thiepval sub-sectors. We had under our control two 18 Pr. Batteries & two 4.5 Hrs. Batteries and we also had attached one Bri Hows. Battery. The month was very quiet as we were rather limited in ammunition in account of the preparation being made for the big advance to take place later. However we supplied a successful raid made by the Lancashire Fusiliers who relieved the enemy trenches & brought back 13 prisoners from whom valuable information was obtained. On May 26th/16 the reorganisation of the 32nd Div Arty was carried out & we handed over two Batteries of Hows (4.5"), one to the 155th Bde (A/155) & one to the 161st Bde (B/164) but the same time took over three Batteries of 18 Prs. namely D/155, D/161, & D/158. Two Hows Batts On Brigade consists now of one 4.5 Hows Batt. & three 18 Pr. Batteries.	

32nd Divisional Artillery

164th BRIGADE.

ROYAL FIELD ARTILLERY.

JUNE 1916

Army Form C. 2118.

WAR DIARY
or
INTELLIGENCE SUMMARY
(Erase heading not required.)

XXXI

June 1916
164th Bde. RFA

Vol 6

Place	Date	Hour	Summary of Events and Information	Remarks and references to Appendices
Albert	June 1916		The early part of the month was very quiet the Batteries not shooting more than was necessary in order to save up ammunition for the big bombardment which was to commence on June 24/16. All the Batteries built their Ammunition dumps for storage before the big battle commenced. The Rue 18 Pr Battery had 5000 Rds at the Guns the 4.5 in Hows Battery had 4000 Rds at the Gun. The Batteries on the 5 June Companies with others in the preliminary bombardment covering a successful raid made by the 11" Border Regiment. Eighteen prisoners were taken on the occasion. On June 24th The Major Battle commenced at 7.30 a.m. + the Batteries were practically shooting for 7 consecutive days shots not at time with great bursts at intervals. One A Battery which was pushed up to within 700 yds of the German front line (or more exactly parapet) were rather badly punished by large Enemy shells, two of their guns were smashed up + every gun pit was hit.	

WAR DIARY
or
INTELLIGENCE SUMMARY

Army Form C. 2118.

(Erase heading not required.)

Place	Date	Hour	Summary of Events and Information	Remarks and references to Appendices
			Meanwhile the Battery carries on firing up to the last enemy bombardment. One then decides to draw them further back so they can be & Officer killed (2L 1st Matthews) & the OC Battery (Capt W.S. Butler) wounded, also 7 gunners killed & 13 wounded. One B Battery has no Signaller Rifles & C Battery 2 wounded & D Batt two wounded. The two latter by a penetration from their own guns. All the guns (less limbers) are replaced before the order overtakes. The Battery are sent up to strength again & new Officer.	

C.D. Salter, Lt. R.F.A.
R.F.A.,
Adjutant, 164 (Rotherham) Brigade R.F.A.

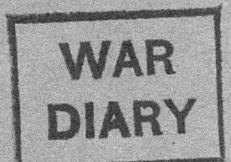

Headquarters,

164th BRIGADE, R.F.A.

(32nd Division)

J U L Y

1 9 1 6

WAR DIARY
INTELLIGENCE SUMMARY

164th Bde, R.F.A.

Place	Date	Hour	Summary of Events and Information	Remarks and references to Appendices
ANCRE Neighbourhood	1/7/16		The Brigade became engaged in the operations in the ANCRE valley, following on the preliminary bombardment of the previous week.	
—"—	9/7/16		2nd Lieut: H.F. MADDERS and 3 O.R. were killed and 5 O.R. wounded. Lieut. Colonel H. ALLCARD, D.S.O, took command of the Group (subsidiary).	
—"—	18/7/16		The Brigade was withdrawn from action to SENLIS	
	19/7/16	8am	Brigade marched from SENLIS to GRUCHES.	Attached from IV. ARMY, to I.st ARMY
	20/7/16		" " GRUCHES to CONCHY SUR CANCHE.	
	21/7/16		" " CONCHY SUR CANCHE to MONCHY-CAYEUX.	
	22/7/16		" " MONCHY-CAYEUX to AMETTES.	
	29/7/16		" " AMETTES to LAPUGNOY	

A.A.Fitzwalter ?Lt. for Lieut. Col.
Commdg. 164th Bde R.F.A.

3 AUG 1916

32nd Divisional Artillery.

164th BRIGADE (Howitzer) R.F.A.

AUGUST 1 9 1 6

164th Bde RFA VOLUME VIII

WAR DIARY
or
INTELLIGENCE SUMMARY

Army Form C. 2118

August 1916

Place	Date	Hour	Summary of Events and Information	Remarks and references to Appendices
LAPUGNOY	1/8/16	—	The Brigade remained in LAPUGNOY until the 4th of August during which time training of various kinds was carried out and the Guns overhauled. During this time the Brigade was visited by Maj. Gen. Mercer RA 1st Army.	
	4/8/16		On this date the four Batteries of the Bde moved up into position to relieve the 8th Div Arty and they all form part of the Left Group under Lt. Col. Chapman D.S.O. (OC 153rd Bde) who commands the Left sector of the 1st Corps front. The Batteries moved into the new position to relieve the right of the 145th, 516th and the Bde marches from LAPUGNOY via LABEUVRIERE — ANNEZIN Road junction E.10d 4.3 — BEUVRY. Their wagon lines were now established at LEQUESNOY.	
	5/8/16		The H.Q.s of 164th Bde moved into BETHUNE	
	26/8/16		The HQs moves in accordance with instruction, to PHILOSOPHE to relieve the 16th Div Arty. Two Batteries of the 32nd Div Arty, namely A/161, C/155, C/164, D/168, D/Bow. relieved Batteries of the 16th Div Arty and were formed into a Group called the HULLUCH Group + commanded by C.C. Allens D.S.O.	

AABath. Lt. Col.
164 Bde RFA

32nd Divisional Artillery.

THE BRIGADE WAS BROKEN UP 17.9.16

164th (Howitzer) BRIGADE R. F. A.

SEPTEMBER 1 9 1 6

164 Brigade, R.F.A WAR DIARY September 1916. Army Form C. 2118.

INTELLIGENCE SUMMARY.

Place	Date	Hour	Summary of Events and Information	Remarks and references to Appendices
PHILOSOPHE	1/9/16		C/164 and D/164 remained in position in action as part of the HULLUCH Group until relieved by the 3rd Division on the nights 15/16th and 16/17th. The Brigade was then diverted owing to the formation of 6 gun batteries, and our batteries reorganized as follows: A/164 ..... {1 Section to A/161 {1 " " B/161 B/164 became B/168 C/164 became A/168 D/164 became D/168 Lt Col. H. Allcard D.S.O. took command of the 155th Brigade R.F.A.	Westward ? for Aug. 164th Bde R.F.A

www.ingramcontent.com/pod-product-compliance
Lightning Source LLC
Chambersburg PA
CBHW081503160426
43193CB00014B/2580